Best Pumpkin Recipes

Diana Loera

Other Books by Diana Loera

12 Extra Special Summer Dessert Fondue Recipes http://tinyurl.com/q7gpgw8

14 Extra Special Winter Holidays Fondue Recipes http://tinyurl.com/lkebggx

Awesome Thanksgiving Leftovers Revive Guide http://tinyurl.com/prxjayg

Best 100 Calorie or Less Dessert Recipes http://tinyurl.com/pn5b46c

Best Bacon Infused Dessert Recipes: 20 Mouthwatering Delicious Desserts Infused with Bacon http://tinyurl.com/owxo3pl

Best Copycat Recipes on the Planet http://tinyurl.com/pcuj24q

Coca Cola Ham, Coca Cola Cake and Other Coca Cola Recipes http://tinyurl.com/pp2wvhz

Party Time Chicken Wing Recipes http://tinyurl.com/ohsc9x8

Summertime Sangria   http://tinyurl.com/oxnlnhm

Please visit www.LoeraPublishingLLC.com to see our complete selection of books.

Topics include cooking, travel, recipes, how to, non- fiction and more.

Table of Contents

Please Read

Nut allergies and other allergies are on the rise. My granddaughter has nut allergies and I am always on the lookout for "hidden" nuts in recipes or when we go out to eat.

One time I ordered a caramel apple sundae in a restaurant for my granddaughter only to find nuts liberally dusted *under* the caramel sauce because the waitress thought it would taste better – no mention of nuts in the menu description so I - foolishly-didn't think to mention that my granddaughter has nut allergies.

So with this being said – some of the recipes in this book contain nuts. I do suggest before serving friends, guests or family members that you check for allergies.

There may be other ingredients that we consider every day that may adversely affect someone. For example, some people do not tolerate dairy well – there is cheese in some recipes.

So with this being said, I urge you to check with family, friends, co-workers, guests etc. before making any recipe.

Thank you for taking the time to read this section.

Introduction

Hello!

Thank you for deciding to read my Best Pumpkin Recipes book.

I love, love, love autumn and anything pumpkin – pumpkin lattes, pumpkin breakfast foods, pumpkin pasta – I could go on and on.

I use dry creamer and in the fall I buy a case of pumpkin flavoured creamer to make it through the seasons when pumpkin flavour isn't on the shelves. Last year, I had to start rationing a bit in mid -summer, cutting the pumpkin creamer with French Vanilla flavoured creamer to make it through until the fall season – and more pumpkin creamer.

Last fall when I was on Facebook shouting my love of the humble pumpkin, someone suggested that I should compile a book of my favorite pumpkin themed recipes.

I ended up creating two, not one, pumpkin themed books.

While some of the recipes in this book are fairly simple, some do require more effort. I love cooking, to me it is like creating art. On a crisp fall day, being able to invest time in a wonderful recipe is very satisfying.

If you work outside the home, you may find the more detailed recipes are best made on the weekend or for a special occasion.

These recipes are not fast food – but they are spectacular and sure to impress.

I'm always on the lookout for more pumpkin recipes – pumpkin lovers know, we can never have enough of pumpkin flavoured recipes.

So with this being said – thank you very much for reading this book. As with all my books – the softcovers are 8 ½ x 11 in size. I hate squinting at recipes and other material in books and I love larger sized books – so I thought you may feel the same.

I like showing photos of recipes but unfortunately, every color photo that I include drives the cost of the book up. I compromised by adding some photographs in but not photos for every recipe so that I can keep the book cost as low as possible. Thank you for understanding.

So, with no further ado – let's take a look at some of my favorite pumpkin recipes and hopefully create a new favorite or two for you.

Sincerely,

Diana

Breakfast

Pumpkin Pie Quinoa Breakfast Casserole

Ingredients:

1 cup water
2 tablespoons pumpkin puree
¼ cup raw quinoa
1 tablespoon maple syrup
1 teaspoon coconut oil
¼ teaspoon gluten-free pure vanilla extract
½ teaspoon ground cinnamon
Pinch ground nutmeg
Pinch ground ginger

Topping:
1 tablespoon coconut oil, melted
1 tablespoon maple syrup
1.5 tablespoon finely ground almond flour
¼ cup pecans, chopped

Instructions:

Preheat oven to 350F and lightly oil a 4 cup casserole dish.

In a small bowl combine all ingredients, minus the topping. Stir until fully mixed, then pour into prepared casserole dish.

Cover with a tight lid and cook for 45-50 minutes.

Meanwhile, combine all topping ingredients. After the 50 minutes are up, remove casserole from oven and sprinkle topping over top of the casserole.

Return to the oven and cook uncovered for another 10-15 minutes, or until golden.

Pumpkin Crepes

Ingredients:

Crepes –
2 cups milk
2 T butter, plus more for cooking
2 eggs
1/2 cup pumpkin puree
1 t vanilla
1 1/2 cups flour
1 T sugar
1/2 t baking powder
1/2 t salt
1 t cinnamon
1/4 t ginger
1/4 t nutmeg
Pinch cloves
Filling -
Brown sugar
Goat cheese
Powdered sugar
Other filling options: maple cream cheese frosting, Nutella, sweetened ricotta, Greek yogurt and honey or whipped cream

Directions:

In a small saucepan over medium-low heat warm the milk and butter until the butter's almost melted. Stir melted completely. Transfer to a medium bowl. Whisk in the eggs, pumpkin puree, and vanilla.

In a large bowl, whisk together flour, sugar, baking powder, salt and spices.

Add the wet ingredients to the dry and whisk until smooth and no lumps remain.

Meanwhile heat a crepe pan or non-stick skillet at medium heat. Melt a teaspoon of butter on the pan. Pour batter into the pan 1/3 cup at a time twirling the pan so the crepe batter thins and spreads out covering the pan. Flip when top is almost set. Remove from pan 30 seconds after flipping and place on a cookie sheet in a 200 degree oven. Melt butter on your pan every few crepes to prevent sticking.

When all crepes are done, sprinkle brown sugar and goat cheese in each crepe, and roll up and place seam side down on a plate. Sprinkle with powdered sugar and serve.

Pumpkin Crepes

Pumpkin Pancakes

Prep time:10 minutes
Cook time: 15 minutes
Total time:25 minutes
 Yield: 4-6

Ingredients:

1 3/4 cups milk
1 cup pumpkin puree
1 egg
2 tablespoons vegetable oil
2 cups all- purpose flour
3 tablespoons brown sugar
2 teaspoons baking powder
1 teaspoon baking soda
2 teaspoons pumpkin spice mix
1/2 teaspoon salt

Directions:

In a large bowl, combine the milk, pumpkin puree, egg and oil.

In another large bowl, stir the flour, brown sugar, baking powder, baking soda, pumpkin spice mix and salt until well blended.

While stirring, slowly add the flour mixture into the pumpkin mixture until blended; try not to over mix the batter. As soon as you see large clumps of flour disappear, stop stirring.

Heat a lightly oiled griddle or frying pan over medium high heat. Add about a ¼ cup of batter for one pancake onto the griddle. Brown on both sides and serve hot with warm maple syrup and butter.

Pumpkin Waffles

Ingredients:

1 cup milk
1/2 cup pumpkin puree
2 eggs
2 tablespoons butter, melted
1/4 cup brown sugar
1/2 teaspoon vanilla
1 1/4 cups flour
1/2 teaspoon baking soda
1/4 teaspoon salt
1/2 teaspoon cinnamon
Maple syrup
Whipped Cream

Directions:

Mix milk, pumpkin, eggs, butter, sugar, and vanilla. In a separate bowl, combine flour, baking soda, salt and cinnamon. Add dry ingredients to wet ingredients and mix well.

Cook waffles according to the instructions for your waffle maker.

Top with syrup and whipped cream

Pumpkin French Toast Bake

Prep time: 10 hours 10 minutes
Cook time: 40 minutes
Total time: 10 hours 50 minutes
Serves: 10

Ingredients:

5 1/2 - 7 1/2 cups 1-inch bread cubes
7 large eggs
2 cups milk
1 tsp vanilla extract
1 1/2 tsp pumpkin pie spice
1/4 cup pumpkin butter (or 1/2 cup pumpkin puree)
3-4 tablespoons brown sugar for topping
Pecans or walnuts (optional)
Instructions

Cut any kind of bread into 1-inch cubes - I recommend a Texas toast variety, but sandwich bread will work, too. Just use enough slice to fill a lightly greased 9x13 baking dish quite full.

In a large bowl, whisk together eggs, milk, vanilla, pumpkin butter and pie spice until well combined.

Pour over bread and push down with a spoon or your hands until it's all soaked and mostly covered. Cover with saran wrap or lid and refrigerate overnight.

In the morning, preheat oven to 350 degrees, uncover and top with brown sugar, additional pumpkin pie spice and nuts (optional). Bake for 35-45 minutes or golden brown and no longer wet.

Serve immediately with maple syrup, honey or agave nectar.

Pumpkin Praline Soft Pretzels

I know this probably should be a snack food but I like making them for a mid -morning breakfast treat. They take a bit of time to make but you'll be thinking about making them again as soon as you take the first bite.

Yield: 7-8 pretzels
Prep time: 30 minutes
Total time: 55 minutes

Ingredients:

PUMPKIN PRALINE

1/2 cup (100 grams) packed light brown sugar
1/4 cup (60 grams) unsalted butter
3 Tablespoons (45 ml) milk (any kind, any fat content)
1 Tablespoon pumpkin puree
1 cup (120 grams) confectioners' sugar

BASIC PRETZEL DOUGH
1 packet Red Star Platinum Yeast (1 packet = 2 and 1/4 teaspoons instant dry yeast)
1 and ½ cups (360 ml) warm water (approximately 110-115F degrees)
1 teaspoon salt
1 Tablespoon (15 grams) packed light brown sugar
4 – 4.25 cups (500-530 grams) all-purpose flour
9 cups (2,160 ml) water
1/2 cup baking soda

TOPPING
2 Tablespoons (30 grams) butter, melted
1/3 cup (42 grams) granulated sugar
1 teaspoon ground cinnamon, 1/2 teaspoon ground cloves, and 1/2 teaspoon ground nutmeg (or you may use pumpkin pie spice)

Directions:

Preheat oven to 425F degrees. Line two large baking sheets with parchment paper or a silicone baking mats. Set aside.

Make the praline topping first: Add the brown sugar, butter, and milk to a small saucepan over medium heat. Continuously whisk the mixture until smooth and bring to a boil. Allow to boil for 1 minute without stirring. Remove from heat and stir in the pumpkin and confectioners' sugar until smooth. Set aside and allow to thicken for at least 20 minutes.

Make the pretzels: Whisk the yeast in 1.5 cups warm water. Allow to almost fully dissolve, about 1 minute. Whisk in the salt and brown sugar until combined. Slowly add the flour 1 cup at a time. Mix with a large spoon until dough is thick and no longer sticky. Do not add too much flour or the pretzels will not be soft. After 3-4 cups of flour, poke the dough with your finger. If it bounces back, it is ready to knead. If not, add a bit more flour.

Turn the dough out onto a floured surface. Knead the dough for 3 minutes and shape into a ball. With a sharp knife, cut into 7-8 sections. Roll each section into a 20-inch rope with an even diameter. Take the ends of the rope and form a giant U shape. Take the ends, twist them, and bring them in towards yourself creating a pretzel shape.

Whisk 9 cups of water and the baking soda together in a large pot. Bring to a boil. Place a pretzel onto a large slotted spatula and dip into the boiling water for 20-30 seconds.   Do not exceed the 30 seconds or your pretzels may have a weirdly metallic taste. The pretzel will float. Lift the pretzel out of the water and allow as much of the excess water to drip off. Place pretzel onto prepared baking sheet. Repeat with the rest of the pretzels.

Bake for 10 minutes. During that time, make the topping by melting the butter in a small bowl. Mix the granulated sugar and spices together in another small bowl. Remove the pretzels from the oven and brush each top with the melted butter and generously sprinkle with the sugar/pumpkin spice mixture. Place back into the oven and bake for another 5 minutes. Remove from the oven and sprinkle with more sugar/pumpkin spice if desired.

Drizzle the praline on top of each pretzel. Serve warm or at room temperature. Pretzels may be stored in an airtight container in the refrigerator for up to 3 days. Unglazed pretzels freeze well, up to 2 months.

Lunch

Pumpkin Cheddar Mac and Cheese

I know at first glance this may sound a bit odd but it is a family favorite at our house in the fall. It definitely is a cold weather comfort food. While I list this recipe under lunch, it also is great for your evening meal.

Prep time: 15 mins
Cook time: 15 mins
Total time: 30 mins
Serves: 6-8 servings

Ingredients
1 pound penne, macaroni or twist type pasta
4 tablespoons butter
3 rounded tablespoons flour
1 cup chicken stock (use vegetable stock if you want to make it vegetarian)
2 tablespoons honey
2 cups milk
½ teaspoon allspice
1 teaspoon ground mustard
Pinch of cayenne pepper- optional- I often omit
Freshly grated nutmeg, to taste
Salt and pepper, to taste
2 cups pumpkin puree
2½ cups shredded extra-sharp cheddar cheese, divided
Sweet paprika, for sprinkling - optional
Chopped parsley, for garnish – again optional, I only garnish if I have fresh parsley in the house

Directions:

Bring a large pot of salted water to a boil. Cook pasta according to package directions until al dente. Drain and reserve.

Meanwhile, melt the butter in a large pan. Whisk in the flour and cook for a minute. Whisk in the chicken (or vegetable) stock and cook until it has reduced down where there is almost no liquid left. Whisk in the honey and the milk. Season with the allspice, mustard, cayenne if you are adding it, nutmeg and salt and pepper. Cook, stirring often, until thickened and it coats the back of a spoon. Taste and adjust the seasonings, if needed.

Preheat the broiler.

Whisk in the pumpkin puree. Stir in 2 cups of the cheese until melted. Combine the pasta and the sauce and transfer to individual casserole dishes, or one large casserole dish. Sprinkle the remaining cheese on top and sprinkle with paprika. Broil until the cheese is melted and bubbling. Garnish with chopped parsley and serve.

Roasted Pumpkin Risotto with Sweet Italian Sausage, Apples and Gruyere
(Serves about 4)

My family loves this dish and it really shouts crisp and cool Autumn days.

Ingredients:

1 small sugar pumpkin, peeled, seeded and diced to ½" cubes
2 medium golden delicious apples, peeled, cored and diced to ½" cubes
1 teaspoon pumpkin pie spice
3 tablespoons olive oil, divided use
½ teaspoons salt
½ teaspoons black pepper
2 tablespoons honey
3 tablespoons butter, divided use
1 small onion, chopped
1 cup Arborio Rice – Look in the Hispanic food aisle at your grocery store if it isn't in with the other rice where you shop
½ cups white wine
4 cups chicken stock, very hot
2 sweet Italian sausage links, casings removed and browned
¼ cup shredded Gruyere cheese
¼ cup shaved Parmesan Cheese
4 leaves fresh sage, chopped

Preparation:

Preheat the oven to 400 degrees, line a baking sheet with foil, and drizzle it with a little olive oil.

In a medium bowl, toss together the cubed pumpkin and the apples with the pumpkin pie spice, salt, pepper, honey and 2 tablespoon of the olive oil, and turn them out onto the foil-lined baking sheet in a single layer.

Place in the oven to roast for about 25-30 minutes until golden brown, stirring them a bit about halfway through to prevent them from burning on the bottom.

While the pumpkin and apples roast, begin the risotto.

Preheat a large, heavy-bottom pan over medium/medium-high heat; once hot, add 2 tablespoons of butter and the remaining tablespoon of olive oil to the hot pan to melt together.

Then add the chopped onion for about 2 minutes until translucent.

Add the Arborio rice and gently stir, making sure to coat all the rice grains in the butter/oil for about a minute or two.

Add the white wine to the rice and onions.

Stir gently, allowing the wine to reduce until almost absorbed, but not quite completely;

Begin adding the hot chicken stock to the rice mixture, about ½ cup to ¾ cup at a time.

Stirring gently to incorporate and allowing the rice to slowly absorb the stock.

Adjust the flame if necessary, so the rice is at a gentle simmer, not bubbling too harshly, as this will evaporate the stock too fast.

Once the first increment of stock is mostly absorbed (about 3 minutes), add another ½ cup – ¾ cup of stock, stirring and allowing it to almost absorb, repeating this process until the rice is soft and creamy, but not mushy—roughly 23 minutes or so total.

Finish the risotto, turn the heat off from under the pan; add in the remaining tablespoon of butter, the grated Gruyere, the shaved Parmesan, the browned sweet Italian sausage, the roasted pumpkin and apples, and about ½ of the chopped sage; gently fold all ingredients together in the pan, and spoon generous portions of the risotto into bowls, and serve immediately, garnishing each serving with an additional sprinkle of the sage, and an additional sprinkle of cheese, if desired.

Pumpkin Ravioli with Brown Butter Sauce and Pecans

This is a great recipe and while the pecans really set this dish off, I always like to mention – ensure guests do not have nut allergies before making this dish

Prep time: 1 hour 30 min

To make 24 ravioli

2 1/2 cup flour
2 egg
1 cup hot water
1/4 teaspoon salt

Ingredients for pumpkin ravioli filling for 24 ravioli
1/2 can pumpkin
2 tablespoons brown sugar
1/8 teaspoon ground nutmeg
Salt and pepper

Ingredients for brown butter sauce:
1 stick butter
2 and 1/2 tablespoons balsamic vinegar
1 and 1/2 tablespoons brown sugar
1/4 cup chopped toasted pecans

To make ravioli dough:

Mix flour with salt.

Stir water with egg until well mixed.

In a bowl, combine flour and egg-water mixture together and mix until well incorporated. Knead the dough until well-textured and firm. The dough should not be too wet or too sticky. It should only stick to itself, but not to your hands. It should not be too dry, either. Make the dough into a ball or disk, wrap with plastic wrap. Let the dough stand for 1 hour at room temperature before using. This allows gluten to work.

To make pumpkin ravioli filling and assemble:

If your pumpkin puree or mashed pumpkin is too watery, drain the pumpkin using a paper towel and a mesh strainer to get rid of any unnecessary liquids.

Mix pumpkin puree with brown sugar and nutmeg. Season filling with salt and pepper.

Unwrap a batch of ravioli dough from plastic, divide in 2 equal parts. Flour working area. Roll out each part of pasta dough very thinly, on a floured surface, using a roller. Make sure to flour the upper portion of pasta dough and the roller to avoid sticking. Lift the rolled dough several times during rolling to make sure it doesn't stick to the counter, and flour working surface with more flour, if necessary.

Flour the ravioli mold. After you have rolled the 2 portions of dough very thinly, place first layer of dough on the ravioli mold, so that it covers all 12 holes.

Place a small portion of ravioli filling into each indentation, making sure not to overfill. The filling should be at the same level or lower as the flat part of the mold. Place second layer of pasta dough on top of filled ravioli.

Using a roller pin, roll across the mold and along the edges to separate ravioli. As you roll the pin, it also removes all air from ravioli, which is very important for ravioli success. By now you should have extra dough hanging off the outside 4 edges of ravioli mold – carefully separate it. Continue rolling the pin along the inside edges of 12 raviolis to separate them from one another: you could also use your fingers to press across the edges to separate ravioli.

Flip ravioli mold to release ravioli. Bring a large pot of water to boil. Boil ravioli for 5 minutes, drain and set aside – to be used with sauce below.

Or, alternatively, if you're not using ravioli right away, place them on a plate or baking sheet in the freezer to freeze. After they are frozen, place them in a plastic bag and keep frozen until needed.

If you're more of a visual person and would like photos that walk you through on how to use this ravioli mold, I have a very detailed tutorial-recipe with photos on how to make ravioli using this mold and another very detailed recipe, also with photos, describing how to use the same ravioli mold.

To make brown butter sauce:

Preheat oven to 350. Toast pecans for 10 minutes until slightly browned, let them cool off and then chop them finely.

Melt butter in a large skillet over medium heat. Cook until butter just begins to brown, about 4 minutes. Do not overcook or the butter will burn. Remove from heat. Mix in balsamic vinegar and brown sugar. Add ravioli to the hot butter sauce, spoon sauce over to coat ravioli. Transfer to plates. Sprinkle with pecans.

Pumpkin Ravioli

Dinner

Creamy Pumpkin Pasta

6 servings

Ingredients:

1 lb penne pasta
2 garlic cloves
2 Tbsp. olive oil
1 cup pumpkin puree
1 cup vegetable broth
1/2 cup heavy cream
1/2 cup milk
1 tsp salt
1/2 tsp nutmeg
1 -2 cup Parmigiano Reggiano cheese depending upon how much you love cheese. You can also substitute Parmesan cheese
1 tsp pepper flakes, optional.

Directions:

Cook pasta according to box instructions.

In a large skillet heat the oil over medium to high heat.

Add the garlic and cook for about 30 seconds, just until fragrant.

Add the pumpkin puree, vegetable broth and mix through.

Add heavy cream, milk, nutmeg and salt and cook over medium heat stirring occasionally for about 5 minutes.

Add the cheese and pepper flakes if using.

Stir, turn off the heat and stir in the pasta.

Serve with additional cheese and pepper flakes on the side.

Pumpkin Rosemary Pasta

Ingredients:

340g/12oz pasta such as shells – I prefer the medium shells but large shells make a beautiful presentation on a plate. Penne pasta can also be used.
1 small pumpkin
2 sprigs rosemary
1 clove garlic
1 shallot
140ml/5fl oz carton double cream
1 tsp Dijon mustard
2 tsp chopped flat leaf parsley
30-55g/1-2oz butter
150ml/¼ pint white wine
½ lemon, juice only
Salt and freshly ground black pepper
Grated parmesan (or similar vegetarian hard cheese), to serve

Directions:

Preheat the oven 190C/375F/Gas 5.

Peel and de-seed the pumpkin. Dice into 2.5cm/1in and place onto an ovenproof sheet.

Chop the rosemary and sprinkle over the pumpkin. Season and drizzle with olive oil.

Place in the oven and cook for 45 minutes.

Cook the pasta in plenty of salted boiling water as per instructions.

Chop the garlic and shallot, gently pan-fry in the butter for about 1 minute.

Add the mustard and wine, bring to the boil. Simmer for 2-3 minutes.

Add the lemon juice, seasoning, cream and finally the parsley.

Drain off the pasta and remove the pumpkin from the oven. Fold into the pasta in a bowl.

Pour over the sauce and mix together. Check seasoning. Serve in a bowl with the parmesan cheese over the top.

Pumpkin Fettuccini Alfredo

Ingredients:

1 teaspoon olive oil
2 tablespoons butter
4 cloves of garlic, minced
1 cup heavy cream
1 cup pumpkin puree
1 teaspoon Herbs de Provence
Salt and pepper, to taste
8 ounces fettuccine, cooked
Freshly grated parmesan, to garnish
Fresh sage, julienne, to garnish

Directions:

Heat oil and butter in a sauce pan with minced garlic and cook until lightly golden and fragrant.

Whisk in cream, pumpkin and spices and let simmer until thoroughly heated and smooth.

Toss with cooked pasta, garnish with parmesan and sage.

Pumpkin and Ricotta Lasagna with Sage, Hazelnuts and Burnt Butter Sauce

Serves 4

Ingredients:

1 box lasagne pasta
1 small Pumpkin
150 grams unsalted butter plus 50 grams butter
1 vanilla bean, scraped
400 grams ricotta
1 egg
Pinch of nutmeg
Salt and pepper to taste
100 grams parmesan cheese
10 sage leaves
20 grams toasted hazelnuts

Directions:

You will need to boil the lasagna sheets of pasta while you are making the sauce. I suggest doing so right after you make the pumpkin puree.

To make the pumpkin puree, peel the pumpkin and diced into 2 inch cubes. Heat the 150 grams of butter in a pan and add the pumpkin once the butter is melted. Add the vanilla bean and scraped seeds and cook the pumpkin until soft enough that you can cut it with a spoon, around 20 minutes. Stir the pumpkin once in a while to make sure that the pumpkin doesn't catch to the bottom of the pan. Once the pumpkin is soft enough, blend or process the pumpkin until smooth. Set aside.

Mix the ricotta, egg and nutmeg together in a bowl. Season with salt and pepper. Set aside Grease a baking pan with some olive oil and lay sheets of cooked pasta to cover the bottom of the pan. Layer a third of the pumpkin puree and top with more of the lasagna sheets.

Top with a third of the ricotta mixture and the cover again with more lasagna sheets.

Now add half of the remaining pumpkin puree and cover with the lasagna sheets. Add half of the remaining ricotta and again, more lasagna sheets. Finally, spread the remaining pumpkin puree and on top of this add the rest of the ricotta. Top with parmesan cheese.

Bake the lasagna in a pre-heated oven at 180c (fan forced) for 30 minutes, or until the cheese is golden brown. Remove from oven.
Add the sage leaves. Top with the toasted hazelnuts.

Pumpkin Ricotta Gnocchi

Prep time: 30 minutes
Cook time: 15 minutes
Yield: Serves 4-8.

Ingredients:

1 cup of puréed cooked pumpkin or winter squash (canned or homemade)
1 cup ricotta (use whole milk for best results)
2 large eggs
2 teaspoons kosher salt
1/4 cup parmesan or pecorino cheese
3-4 cups all-purpose flour
2-3 teaspoons minced fresh sage
1/4 cup unsalted butter
Black pepper to taste
Truffle salt to taste (optional)

To make your own pumpkin purée, cut a small sugar pumpkin (or other winter squash) in half.
Scoop out the seeds and strings. Lay the pumpkin face down on a foil-lined baking sheet.
Bake at 350°F for 45 minutes to an hour, until soft. Allow to cool, then scoop out the flesh and mash with a fork.

Directions:

Mix the pumpkin puree, ricotta, parmesan, eggs and salt together in a large bowl.
 Add 2 cups of the flour and mix well with your hands.
The dough should be very sticky and impossible to work.
Add another half cup of flour and mix in — you want the dough to still be pretty sticky, but pliable enough to shape into a large log.
If it's not, keep adding a little flour at a time until you can get a soft dough that will be rollable.
It should never require more than 4 cups of flour.
Cover the dough with a damp towel.

Bring a large pot of water to a boil.

Let this simmer while you make the gnocchi.

To make the gnocchi, spread some flour on a large work surface and have more flour ready.

Cut the dough log into four equal pieces.

Take one piece and cut it in half. Roll the piece of dough into a snake about 1/2 inch thick, then cut it into pieces about the thickness of a fork.

Dust the gnocchi with a little flour, then use one finger to push the dumpling up onto the tines of a fork.

Let the gnocchi drop back to the work surface. This does two things: It makes the dumpling a little thinner and lighter, and it creates depressions and ridges that sauce can hold onto.

Repeat this process with the other piece of dough and then, using a metal spatula, gently pick up a few gnocchi at a time and drop them into the water. Increase the heat to a rolling boil. Boil these gnocchi until they float, then remove them with a slotted spoon.

Lay the cooked gnocchi on a baking sheet and toss with a little olive oil so they don't stick together.

Now go back to the next big chunk of dough and repeat the process.

It is important to boil gnocchi in small batches so they don't stick to each other.

When all the gnocchi are made, heat the butter over medium-high heat until it stops frothing.

Add enough gnocchi to the pan to cover it in one layer.

Do not let them stack up on each other.

Let them fry undisturbed for 90 seconds.

Sprinkle half the sage over the pan.

Cook for another minute, then turn out onto plates.

Repeat with the remaining gnocchi.

If you have to do this in several batches, keep the finished gnocchi on baking sheet in the oven set on Warm.

Serve as soon as they're all done, dusted with black pepper and the truffle salt.

Pumpkin Rosemary Gnocchi

Balsamic Glazed Pumpkin with Walnuts

I had this dish at a restaurant in Boston several years ago and when I came across this recipe, I was more than delighted.

Ingredients: (serves 2-3 as a small side)

3 cups sliced (approx.) pumpkin/butternut squash
1 tablespoon olive oil
1/2 teaspoon cumin seeds
1 whole red dry chili pepper
1 teaspoon crushed red pepper, or to taste
1.5 tablespoon balsamic vinegar
1/2 cup walnuts, broken and lightly toasted
Salt to taste
Chopped fresh herbs (your choice) for garnish

Direction:

Peel and slice the pumpkin/butternut squash into 1/4 inch thick small slices.

Heat oil in a pan and add the cumin and the whole red chili pepper; when the cumin sizzles and the red chili pepper turns a shade darker, add the sliced pumpkin/butternut squash and salt.
Cook at high heat while tossing them in the pan until they are half cooked and browned on both sides.

Add the balsamic vinegar, crushed pepper and the toasted walnuts and reduce the heat to medium.

Cook while tossing and scraping off the bottom of the pan until the slices are cooked and thoroughly glazed.

Garnish with your favorite herb. I use fresh cilantro or fresh sage depending which I have on hand.

Soups

Smoked Pumpkin Chili

Ingredients:

1 medium to large cooking onion, chopped
3 large cloves of garlic, chopped
1 tablespoon olive oil
2 cans (or one large can) of dark kidney beans, drained and rinsed.
1 can of low-sodium corn kernels, drained and rinsed
1 large (28 ounce) can whole peeled tomatoes, keep the juice
1 can pumpkin puree
1 cup vegetable broth (or beer of choice)
1 tablespoon smoked paprika (or regular)
1 teaspoon black pepper
1/2 to 1 teaspoon salt
10 to 15 sage leaves (optional)

Directions:

In a large saucepan, heat the olive oil over medium-high heat and add the onions and garlic. Cook until onions are tender.

Pour in the pumpkin puree and vegetable broth (or beer). Mix. Pour in the can of whole tomatoes (with the juice). Mix again.

Then add the kidney beans and corn kernels. Season with the paprika, black pepper, and salt.

Bring mixture to a boil, stirring occasionally. You'll want to use a spatula or mixing spoon to crush the whole tomatoes a bit. Keep them chunky, but try to crush each one a couple times to distribute evenly.

Then lower the heat to a simmer and cover. Cook for 45 minutes. Again, stir occasionally.

Add in the sage leaves.

Cook at a low simmer for another 15 minutes.

Remove from heat and serve.

Smokey Pumpkin Quinoa Chili

Serves: 5-6

Ingredients:

1 medium onion, chopped
1 large red bell pepper, seeded and chopped
1 large clove garlic, minced
12 ounces Chicken Sausage, casings removed
1 teaspoon chili powder
1 teaspoon creole seasoning
1/2 teaspoon garlic powder
1 teaspoon liquid hickory smoke
2 cups chicken or beef stock
1 cup pumpkin puree
1 cup cooked quinoa

Directions:

In a large non-stick skillet, sauté the onion, bell pepper, and garlic until they begin to soften.

Add the chicken sausage to the skillet and break up thoroughly as it cooks through.

As the sausage cooks, add the seasonings and the liquid smoke and mix thoroughly.

Meanwhile, in a small bowl, whisk together the chicken stock and the pumpkin puree.

Once the sausage has cooked completely, add in the pumpkin/stock mixture and the quinoa. Stir together thoroughly.

Simmer on medium heat until completely heated through.

Serve garnished with sliced green onions and a drizzle of coconut milk.

Creamy Pumpkin-Peanut Soup

Prep Time: 10 minutes
Cooking Time: 20 minutes

Ingredients:

2 tsp vegetable oil
1 small onion, chopped (1 1/4 cups)
3 cloves garlic, smashed
1/4 tsp ground turmeric
1/2 tsp paprika
1/2 tsp chili pepper flakes
1 can solid-pack pumpkin puree (15 oz)
1 1/2 cups low-sodium chicken or vegetable broth
1 jar roasted red peppers (7 oz), drained, 1 tablespoon chopped and reserved for garnish
1/3 cup smooth reduced-fat natural peanut butter
1 tsp sugar
1/2 tsp salt
1/4 tsp freshly ground black pepper
1 Tbsp. fresh lemon juice
1/4 cup reduced-fat sour cream
2 Tbsp. chopped roasted peanuts
2 Tbsp. chopped scallion greens

Directions:

Heat oil in a 4-quart saucepan over medium-high heat. Add onion and cook, stirring, until golden, about 10 minutes. Add garlic and cook an additional 2 minutes.

Add turmeric, paprika, and chili flakes; stir. Add pumpkin puree, broth, peppers, and peanut butter; whisk to incorporate and bring to a boil.

Reduce heat, simmer for 5 minutes, then stir in sugar, salt, pepper, and lemon juice.

Transfer to a blender or food processor and puree until smooth.

Divide among 4 bowls and garnish with sour cream, peanuts, reserved chopped peppers, and scallion greens.

Creamy Pumpkin Peanut Soup

Salad

Roasted Pumpkin and Pomegranate Salad with Pumpkin Seed Oil Vinaigrette

This salad makes a statement on the table. I've had numerous guests compliment not only how this salad looked but how it tasted. Make copies of this recipe beforehand as your guests will probably ask you for a copy.

Prep Time: 15 minutes
Cooking Time: 30 minutes

Ingredients:

3 cups pumpkin, cut into 1-inch cubes
2 tsp extra-virgin olive oil
1/4 tsp salt
1/4 tsp pepper
6 cups mixed winter salad greens
1/2 cup pomegranate seeds
8 tsp lightly toasted pumpkin seeds
1/4 cup crumbled goat cheese

Vinaigrette: (makes 1/2 cup)
3 Tbsp. pure pumpkin-seed oil (available in health-food stores and specialty markets)
2 Tbsp. champagne vinegar
3 Tbsp. orange juice
1 tsp Dijon mustard
1 small chopped shallot (1 Tbsp.)
1 tsp honey
1/4 tsp salt
1/4 tsp pepper

Directions:

Preheat oven to 400°F. Toss pumpkin with olive oil, salt, and pepper and arrange in one layer on a lipped baking sheet. Roast until pumpkin is tender-firm and edges are caramelized, about 30 minutes. Remove from oven and let cool completely.

Combine all vinaigrette ingredients in a small jar with a tight-fitting lid and shake until dressing emulsifies and has a creamy appearance.

Divide the greens evenly among 4 salad plates. Scatter 1/2 cup roasted pumpkin, 1 tablespoon pomegranate seeds, 2 teaspoons pumpkin seeds, and 1 tablespoon goat cheese on top of each plate of greens.

Drizzle with 2 tablespoons vinaigrette.

Serve immediately.

If possible, serve on plates that accent the colors in this salad or use salad charger plates to make this presentation really pop.

Creamy Pumpkin Roasted Potato Salad

Ingredients:

Roast:
3 cups tiny potatoes, halved and quartered
2 Tbsp. olive oil
1/4 tsp truffle salt (or regular salt)
1/2 tsp fine black pepper
1 tsp parsley flakes
Fresh herb sprigs optional (I used a sprig of thyme)

Pumpkin Salad Sauce:
1 cup pumpkin puree
1/3 cup Mayonnaise
1 Tbsp. maple syrup
2 Tbsp. dried parsley flakes
1/2 tsp fine black pepper
2 Tbsp. apple cider vinegar
Salt to taste

Fold in:
1 cup diced sweet onion

Directions:

Toss sliced potatoes with the roasting ingredients.

You can add any fresh herb sprigs you'd like (optional).

Roast at 400 degrees for about 20 minutes– or until the potatoes are tender.

Whip together the pumpkin salad sauce ingredients

Toss the roasted potatoes with the onions.

Then fold the pumpkin sauce into the roasted potato/onion mixture.

Serve warm or place in fridge to cool if you'd like to serve chilled. The salad sauce will thicken when chilled.

Dips

Fall Pumpkin Dip Recipe

PREP TIME: 10 minutes
TOTAL TIME: 10 minutes
Serves: Makes about 3 cups.

Ingredients:
8 oz. cream cheese
1 cup light brown sugar
¾ teaspoon ground ginger
½ teaspoon ground nutmeg
2 teaspoon cinnamon
1 15 oz. can pumpkin puree

Instructions:

In a food processor (or in a bowl by hand) pulse the cream cheese until smooth.

Add next 4 ingredients (light brown sugar, ground ginger, ground nutmeg, ground cinnamon) to food processor and blend well.

Transfer cream cheese mixture into a bowl, add the pumpkin puree and mix well. Refrigerate until served.

Pumpkin Hummus Recipe

Ingredients:
8 oz. dry garbanzo beans
4 cups water
1 teaspoon salt
1 – 15 oz. can pumpkin puree
1/4 cup tahini paste
Juice of 1 lemon
1/4 cup olive oil
1 teaspoon cumin

Directions:

Rinse beans and check for any bad beans and remove.

Add water to beans and let soak 4 – 6 hours or overnight.

Place beans and their water in a saucepan and bring to a boil over medium heat.

Let simmer over medium low heat until tender, about an hour.

Add cooked beans and their water to a food processor. Add canned pumpkin puree, tahini paste, lemon juice and cumin.

Pulse until combined.

Then turn on food processor and stream in olive oil.

Blend until hummus is creamy.

Serve with pita chips or carrot sticks.

Skinny Pumpkin Nutella Dip

This is definitely the quickest recipe in this book. It is a good last minute entertaining recipe. Great to bring to office potlucks too.

Ingredients

1/2 cup Nutella , softened just a little in the microwave
1/2 cup of pumpkin (100% pure pumpkin puree)
1 8 oz container of Lite Cool Whip

Directions:

Whisk together the Nutella and the pumpkin and then gently fold it into the cool whip until completely combined.

I like to serve with graham crackers or the honey graham bear crackers.

Pumpkin Chocolate Chip Cookie Dough Dip

Serves: 1 cup

Ingredients:

4 Tbsp. unsalted butter
1/4 cup brown sugar
1/2 tsp vanilla
4 ounces cream cheese, softened
1/2 cup powdered sugar
1/2 cup pumpkin puree
1/4 tsp cinnamon
1/4 tsp clove
1/4 tsp salt
1/2 cup chocolate chips

Directions:

In a small saucepan, melt the butter. Whisk in brown sugar until it dissolves and starts to bubble.

Remove from the heat and whisk in vanilla. Set aside.

In a large bowl, cream together the cream cheese and sugar until smooth.

Beat in the melted butter mixture until smooth.

Beat in the pumpkin, cinnamon, clove, and salt until smooth.

Stir in the chocolate chips.

Serve with graham crackers or gingersnaps.

Thank you for taking the time to read through my favorite pumpkin recipes. I hope that you've found a new favorite or two.

If you are a real pumpkin lover, I also created a book of my favorite pumpkin drink and dessert recipes.

You'll find it on Amazon, on my website www.LoeraPublishing.com and on www.Swingbellys.com

I am constantly looking for new recipes and new topics to create books. Currently, I have three other recipe books in the works to be released later this year.

Thank you again for taking the time to read my book.

Sincerely,

Diana Loera